AGAINST THE ODDS

Marie Curie

Claire Throp

raintree
a Capstone company — publishers for children

Raintree is an imprint of Capstone Global Library Limited, a company incorporated in England and Wales having its registered office at 7 Pilgrim Street, London EC4V 6LB – Registered company number: 6695582

www.raintreepublishers.co.uk
myorders@raintreepublishers.co.uk

Edited by Linda Staniford and Jennifer Besel
Designed by Philippa Jenkins and Tim Bond
Picture research by Tracy Cummins
Production by Helen McCreath
Originated by Capstone Global Library Limited
Printed and bound in China by LEO

ISBN 978 1 406 29755 3
19 18 17 16 15
10 9 8 7 6 5 4 3 2 1

British Library Cataloguing in Publication Data
A full catalogue record for this book is available from the British Library.

Acknowledgements
We would like to thank the following for permission to reproduce photographs: Alamy: Everett Collection Historical, 20, INTERFOTO, 8, 15, 21; Corbis: Bettmann, 13, 24, Hulton-Deutsch Collection, 43, Science Faction 38, Stefano Bianchetti, 16; Getty Images: APIC, 31, Couprie/Hulton Archive, 28, Keystone-France/Gamma-Keystone, 40, Oxford Science Archive/Print Collector, 37, Popperfoto, 34, Roger Viollet, 26; Musée Curie/coll. ACJC: 30; Science Source: Cover, Emilio Segrè Visual Archives /American Institute of Physics, 39, SPL 12; Shutterstock: Anton_Ivanov, 27; Thinkstock: Photos.com, 5, 6, 7, 9, 10, 11, 14, 23, 33, 36, 41; Wikimedia: Paul Nadar, 19, www.imagebank. sweden.se, Gösta Florman / The Royal Library: 18.

Every effort has been made to contact copyright holders of material reproduced in this book. Any omissions will be rectified in subsequent printings if notice is given to the publisher.

Contents

Who was Marie Curie? 4

What was Marie Curie's upbringing like? 6

What was Marie Curie's research about?......12

What was Marie Curie's life like after
  winning the Nobel Prize?.................20

What difficulties did Marie Curie face
  in 1911 and 1912? 26

What did Marie Curie do during
  World War I?................................32

What did Marie Curie do after
  World War I?................................ 36

What happened in the last years
  of Marie Curie's life?.........................40

What was Marie Curie's legacy? 42

Timeline................................. 44

Glossary 45

Find out more...47

Index.. 48

Some words are shown in bold, **like this**. You can find out what they mean by looking in the glossary.

Who was Marie Curie?

Marie Curie was a scientist. Along with her husband, Pierre, she discovered two new **radioactive elements**: polonium and radium. Curie was also responsible for seeing that there was a possible use for radium in treating cancer.

A life of firsts

The Nobel Prize is a highly respected scientific award that is presented each year. Marie Curie became the first person to win two Nobel Prizes. What made this even more impressive is that her prizes were won in different subjects – the first in **Physics** and the second in **Chemistry**.

Marie Curie later became the first woman to teach at the Sorbonne, a well-known university in Paris, France. In 1995, she became the first woman to be buried at the Panthéon in Paris, a building in which usually only important French men were buried.

Not an easy life

Marie Curie's life was a struggle at times. It began in poverty in Poland and money – or lack of it – was a problem for much of her life. Another major problem for Curie was the fact that she was a woman. In the late 19th and early 20th centuries, higher education in many countries was only for men. Science in particular was not seen as a suitable subject for women. Once Curie moved to France, the fact that she was not French also sometimes counted against her.

A FAMILY OF NOBEL PRIZE WINNERS

Marie and Pierre's eldest daughter, Irène, later won a Nobel Prize herself. Along with her husband, Frédéric, she won the Prize in Chemistry in 1935.

Marie Curie is one of the best-known scientists in the world.

What was Marie Curie's upbringing like?

Marie Curie was born Maria Sklodowska in Warsaw (then part of the Russian Empire, but now in Poland), on 7 November 1867. Maria was the youngest of five children – she had three sisters and one brother. Her parents were teachers and made sure that their daughters were as well educated as their son. This was unusual at the time. Boys were expected to get a job when they grew up whereas girls were supposed to get married, have children and stay at home to look after their family. This often meant that the education of girls was not seen to be important.

Maria (centre) is seen here with her brother and sisters.

Maria's mother died in May 1878. She was 42 years old.

Maria got her love of science from her father, Wladislaw, who was a maths and physics teacher. At the time, Warsaw was ruled by the Russian Empire, which greatly angered Maria's father. His feelings caused him to lose a good teaching position. The family were very poor. Zosia, Maria's eldest sister, died of a disease called typhus when Maria was only eight. Maria's mother, Bronislawa, died from a disease called tuberculosis two years later, when Maria was 10.

School

Maria's headteacher had suggested to Maria's father that he hold her back a year. Although Maria was top of the class, she was very sensitive. Instead, Wladislaw pulled her out of that school and sent her to a Russian-run school that focused on extremely clever children. In 1883, Maria **graduated** top of her class in secondary school at the young age of 15.

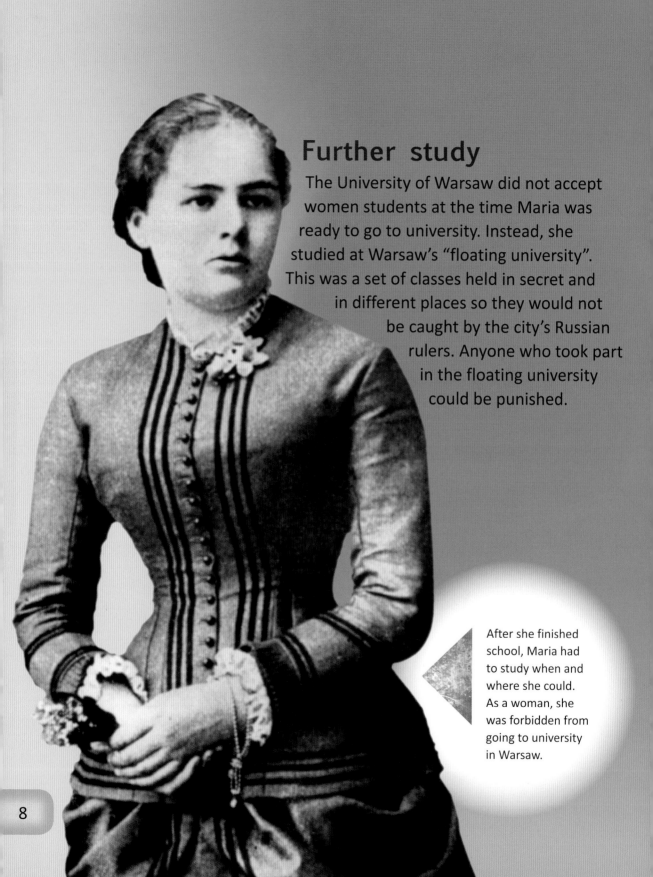

Further study

The University of Warsaw did not accept women students at the time Maria was ready to go to university. Instead, she studied at Warsaw's "floating university". This was a set of classes held in secret and in different places so they would not be caught by the city's Russian rulers. Anyone who took part in the floating university could be punished.

After she finished school, Maria had to study when and where she could. As a woman, she was forbidden from going to university in Warsaw.

Maria and her sister Bronya knew they had to study abroad if they wanted to gain **degrees**, but they had no money. Maria worked as a **tutor** and **governess** for five years from the age of 18 while Bronya studied at medical school in Paris, France. As soon as Bronya was earning she would help to pay for Maria's degree.

Studying at the Sorbonne

In 1891, Maria finally made it to Paris. When she arrived to sign in at the Sorbonne, a top French university, she wrote the French version of her name – Marie – rather than Maria. From then on, she called herself Marie. She had very little money and her health began to suffer as she tried to survive on just tea or cocoa and bread and butter.

Marie had to work hard to catch up with her fellow students, as her education at the floating university did not match the level of education she would need at an ordinary university. However, she still managed to graduate top of her class in physics in July 1893. She was given money from a scholarship for outstanding Polish students, which allowed her to complete a second degree in maths in 1894.

Maria (left) is seen here with her sister Bronya in 1886.

How did Marie meet Pierre Curie?

In 1894, Marie met Pierre Curie, a **professor** at the School of Physics. One of her professors had arranged funding for her to investigate the magnetic properties of steel. Pierre arranged a small area of his **laboratory** for Marie where he worked, at the Municipal School of Industrial Physics and Chemistry.

Who's who

Pierre Curie
(1859–1906)

Pierre Curie was born in Paris in 1859. His father was a doctor and decided he would teach Pierre at home rather than send him to school. After gaining a degree in physics at the young age of 18, Pierre became a laboratory assistant at the Sorbonne. Along with his brother, Jacques, he carried out **research** on crystals and electricity. In 1882, Pierre Curie was made a supervisor at the Municipal School of Industrial Physics and Chemistry. There, he researched the magnetism of substances at different temperatures.

Marriage, work and children

Marie had planned to return to Poland after completing her degrees, but she fell in love with Pierre and he persuaded her to stay in Paris. In July 1895, they got married. Marie continued her **research** on steel for the next two years. She stopped in order to have a daughter, Irène, in September 1897. After Pierre's father lost his wife to breast cancer shortly after Irène's birth, he moved in with the Curies to look after Irène.

"It became a serious problem how to take care of our little Irène and of our home without giving up my scientific work. [This] would have been very painful to me, and my husband would not even think of it."

Marie Curie

The Curies spent their honeymoon cycling around France.

What was Marie Curie's research about?

Marie Curie wanted a new project so that she could gain a doctorate in science. A doctorate was the highest level of degree and it was something that no woman had achieved before. Curie was **inspired** by Wilhelm Roentgen's discovery of **X-rays** and Henri Becquerel's discovery of rays from an element called uranium.

Who's who

Wilhelm Roentgen
(1845–1923)

Wilhelm Roentgen was born in Germany, but his family moved to the Netherlands when he was three years old. As he grew up, he became interested in physics. In 1869, he gained his degree in physics from the University of Zurich. By 1875, he was a professor. He is most famous for his discovery of X-rays in 1895. He used his wife's hand to demonstrate the way the rays showed up the bones in her hand on a **photographic plate**.

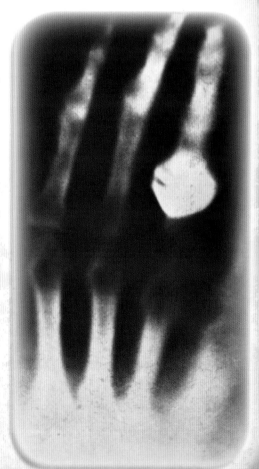

Radioactivity

The rays discovered by Becquerel were not as well known as Roentgen's X-rays, but they fascinated Curie. Some years before, Pierre Curie and his brother, Jacques, had invented a machine that could measure very low levels of electricity in the air. Using this machine, Curie measured the **currents** passing through air that had been hit by uranium rays. She eventually formed the idea that the rays given out by uranium came from the make-up of its **atoms**. She came up with the term "radioactivity" to describe this. Measuring radioactivity became a new way of discovering elements.

Marie Curie spent many hours in the lab, working on her research.

13

An unknown element

Marie Curie studied the **radiation** of compounds known to contain radioactive elements. She discovered that some uranium and thorium compounds had stronger radiation than uranium. This could only mean that an unknown element in each compound had more radiation than uranium or thorium. Pierre now stopped his own research to help Curie in her experiments.

Telling the world

In July 1898, the Curies published their findings: they had discovered a new radioactive element that they called polonium. A second element – radium – was revealed in December. This was groundbreaking work. They found that polonium and radium showed far more radioactivity than uranium and thorium.

The Curies used this machine to help them work out how radiation affected the electrical conductivity of air.

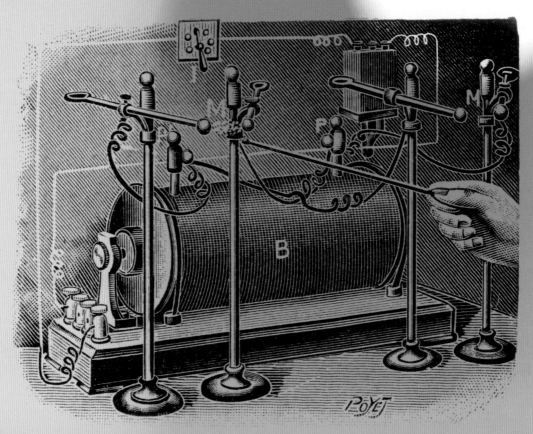

Curie called the lab "this miserable old shed".

A miserable old shed...

The Curies moved into a new lab – an abandoned shed, which had been used by the School of Medicine. The lab was very hot in summer, freezing in winter and the glass roof leaked! However, there was space for the many tonnes of pitchblende required for their research.

Isolating the elements

Not everyone in the scientific world believed that the Curies had discovered two new elements. To prove their existence, the elements would need to be **isolated**. This meant they would need to be separated from other elements into their pure form. The Curies worked with **minerals** called pitchblende and chalcolite. Pitchblende is made up of 30 different elements. Various chemical processes were used to separate the elements. They might dissolve one particular element in acid, for example, leaving the other elements behind. Many separations had to take place until only the element they wanted was left.

NAMING ELEMENTS

Radium was named after the Latin for "ray". Polonium was named after Poland, the country of Marie Curie's birth.

This is a drawing showing the Curies in their laboratory in 1905.

Time and money problems

It took Curie three years to isolate a tenth of a gram of pure radium chloride. She never succeeded in isolating polonium, however. This was because radioactive elements decay over time. Each has what is known as a **half-life** – the amount of time it takes for its radioactivity to reduce in strength by half. Polonium's half-life is only 138 days, so by the time Curie had made all the chemical processes needed to isolate polonium, it was too late; it had decayed and disappeared.

Experiments were costly, and soon the Curies needed more money. In spring 1900, the University of Geneva in Switzerland asked Pierre Curie to be Professor of Physics and offered Marie Curie a job too. They would also be given a well-equipped laboratory. Eventually, though, Pierre Curie refused the job. He did not want to leave France, and he'd finally been offered a professorship at the Sorbonne thanks to Henri Poincaré, a French mathematician and scientist who greatly admired the Curies' work. Marie Curie, meanwhile, got a paid job as a **lecturer** at a teacher training school for women at Sèvres.

However, more hours teaching meant less time for research. Also, there was no lab provided with the job, so the Curies had to continue their research at the old shed.

Health problems

Pierre Curie's health was failing and Marie Curie had lost 9 kilograms (20 pounds) in weight while they'd been doing research. Both had damaged their fingertips handling radioactive materials. No link between their health problems and radium was made at this stage, however.

A FIRST FOR MARIE CURIE

Marie Curie was the first woman to teach at the teacher training school in Sèvres.

Nobel Prize winners

The Curies were joint winners with Henri Becquerel of the Nobel Prize in Physics in 1903. However, Marie Curie nearly missed out.

Charles Bouchard, a doctor, had first **nominated** the Curies in 1902, but they had not won. In 1903, four scientists put forward the names of Pierre Curie and Henri Becquerel, but not Marie Curie. This was even though three of the four scientists had been involved in Curie's work, so they knew that she had played a huge role in the discovery of polonium and radium.

THE NOBEL PRIZE

Industrialist Alfred Nobel died in December 1896, leaving a will that said his fortune should be given out as prizes for outstanding achievements in Physics, Chemistry, Literature, Medicine and Peace. The Nobel Prize was first awarded in 1901.

Who's who

Henri Becquerel
(1852–1908)

Antoine Henri Becquerel was born in Paris. His father and grandfather were both well-known scientists. Becquerel worked as an engineer for the Department of Bridges and Highways before eventually becoming Professor of Physics at the École Polytechnique. In 1896, he accidentally discovered what Marie Curie later called radioactivity. Before he started an experiment involving uranium salts wrapped in black material and placed between photographic plates, he noticed the image of the salts had already appeared on the photographic plate. He realized that it must be the result of rays similar to X-rays coming from the uranium.

The problem was that women scientists were not respected at that time. In the end, only the involvement of Swedish mathematician Magnus Goesta Mittag-Leffler, a supporter of women scientists, allowed Marie Curie to get recognition for her work. He wrote to Pierre Curie, who insisted that it was Marie Curie's research.

What was Marie Curie's life like after winning the Nobel Prize?

When people come up with a new idea or way of making something, such as the way of finding radium discovered by the Curies, they can patent the idea. This allows them to prove that the idea is theirs. Any money that is made from selling the idea would be paid to the owner of the patent. Unfortunately, the Curies didn't patent their method of finding radium. They felt that getting a patent would take up valuable time and money, and it didn't seem likely that radium would make much money.

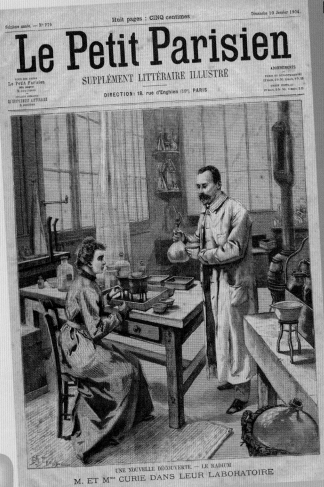

UNE NOUVELLE DÉCOUVERTE. — LE RADIUM
M. ET Mᵐᵉ CURIE DANS LEUR LABORATOIRE

However, radium was becoming popular as a cure-all – everything from cream to prevent the signs of ageing to toothpaste for whitening teeth. So, although a large industry grew up around radium, the Curies did not benefit financially.

However, the Curies were now famous and they found that the demands on their time from people wanting to interview them meant that their research had almost stopped.

Articles about the Curies appeared in magazines around the world.

Marie Curie was thrilled to give birth to a second daughter in 1904. Irène now had a sister, Ève.

A mix of emotions

In August 1903, Curie had finally finished her doctorate. She was also five months pregnant. After a three-week cycling holiday with her husband, she lost her baby. Not long afterwards, one of Bronya's children died from disease. Pierre Curie was also suffering. He sometimes felt too weak even to dress himself.

Then, in December 1904, the Curies' second daughter, Ève, was born. Curie's feelings of despair lifted and she enjoyed being with her new baby.

"I had grown so accustomed to the idea of the child that I am absolutely desperate and cannot be consoled [comforted]."

From a letter written by Marie Curie to her sister Bronya about losing her baby, 25 August 1903

Tragedy

On 19 April 1906, Pierre Curie was killed in an accident. He slipped on a wet street going to the library and a heavy wagon ran over him, killing him instantly. The police first informed the head of Pierre Curie's department at the Sorbonne, Paul Appell. Marie Curie didn't hear about the tragedy until the evening, when she returned from a day out. She then felt guilty because her husband had wanted her to go to the lab with him. She wondered whether he would be alive had she gone with him.

A few days after Pierre Curie's death, Curie began to write a diary. She kept it for about a year. She wrote to her husband as though he were reading it.

Curie was also told by Pierre Curie's brother, Jacques, that the French government had offered to support her family by giving her a pension. Curie refused, saying she could support her family herself.

"Everything is over, Pierre is sleeping his last sleep beneath the earth; it is the end of everything, everything, everything."

Marie Curie

Professor at the Sorbonne

Marie Curie threw herself into work in the lab just one day after her husband's funeral. Less than a month after the funeral, Curie was given the role of professor at the Faculty of Sciences, which her husband had held – she was the first woman to hold the position. It took two more years for her to be given a full professorship, though.

 Marie Curie is seen here with her daughters after the death of Pierre Curie.

All change

In the summer of 1906, Marie Curie, her daughters and her father-in-law moved to Sceaux, an area near Paris where Pierre Curie's family used to live. Pierre and his mother were both buried there.

Life after Pierre Curie's death was difficult for Marie. She continued working while her father-in-law looked after the children.

On 5 November 1906, Curie gave her first lecture at the Sorbonne. Hundreds of people packed into the hall to hear her speak. Many thought they would see tears from Curie, but she remained in control and simply described the developments in physics over the previous 10 years. While it thrilled Curie to be teaching at the Sorbonne, she suffered with the thought that it was only because her husband was no longer alive.

Fighting Lord Kelvin

It took several years of Curie's experiments to fight the suggestion of another scientist, Lord Kelvin, that radium was not an element but a compound. This proposal presented a threat to the whole idea of radioactivity, so Curie worked hard to show that it was false.

In 1910, Pierre Curie's father died, which meant the children then had to be looked after by governesses. They still did not see much of their mother.

"You would have been happy to see me as a professor at the Sorbonne, and I myself would have so willingly done it for you, but to do it in your place, my Pierre, could one dream of a thing more cruel?"

Marie Curie writing in her diary

CURIE SCHOLARSHIPS

American steel-manufacturer and **philanthropist** Andrew Carnegie started the Curie Scholarships, which allowed talented young scientists to research full-time in Curie's lab. They helped on some of Curie's experiments so that she was free to work on others.

What difficulties did Marie Curie face in 1911 and 1912?

In November 1910, Curie decided to put herself forward for the open seat at the French **Academy** of Sciences. The Academy had a lot of control over the way French science was organized. She was up against Édouard Branly, a radio pioneer.

Who's who

Édouard Branly
(1844–1940)

Édouard Branly was born in Amiens, France. Branly was best known for his work in wireless telegraphy, a way of communicating across long distances. One of his inventions, the coherer, helped Marconi to develop his system of wireless telegraphy. Branly was nominated for a Nobel Prize three times but never won.

The Institute of France has five separate academies, including the Academy of Science.

In the run-up to the vote, the newspapers were full of the story of whether a woman would be allowed into the Academy. Some newspapers were supportive of Curie, calling her France's best-known physicist. Other papers pointed out that Curie was Polish, not French. They also suggested that she was Jewish, at a time when most French people were Catholic. In fact, her mother had been Catholic , but Curie was not religious at all. Branly was a French Catholic, which counted in his favour.

The vote

In January 1911, the Academy voted against Curie becoming a member. The vote was 30 to Branly and 28 to Curie. It was so close that another vote was held: should women ever be allowed to join the Academy? The vote was 90 to 52 against. As one Academy member, Emile Hilaire Amagat, said: "Women cannot be part of the Institute of France."

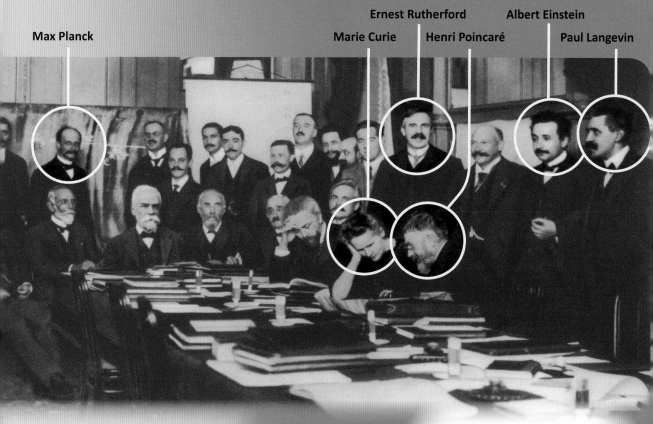

Max Planck

Marie Curie

Ernest Rutherford

Henri Poincaré

Albert Einstein

Paul Langevin

The Solvay Conference

The Solvay **Conference** in Brussels in November 1911 was the first of a series of physics and chemistry conferences involving the best scientists of the time, including Curie. She was in bad health at the time, often complaining of headaches. This was mainly a result of working with radioactive substances, but there was another factor.

During 1910–1911, Curie had been having a relationship with a married man called Paul Langevin. Rumours about their relationship turned into scandal during the conference. Curie's reputation was ruined.

Despite this, Curie discussed the international standard for radium with other scientists. She had been asked to create the measurement for radium. It became known as the Curie.

Marie Curie attended the Solvay Conference in 1911. She is seen here talking to Henri Poincaré. Standing on the far right are Albert Einstein and Paul Langevin.

At the Solvay Conference, Marie Curie was the only woman among 23 well-known male scientists, including Albert Einstein, Max Planck and Ernest Rutherford.

Another Nobel Prize

During the conference, Curie heard she had won the Nobel Prize in Chemistry for her work on radioactivity. This made her the first person to win two Nobel Prizes. Some scientists at the conference thought this unfair because she had been given both prizes for her work on radioactivity. However, most believed that it was deserved after her years of research.

A front-page report in French newspaper *Le Temps* on the Nobel Prize focused on the winner for Literature, Maurice Maeterlinck. Curie was not mentioned. This was a huge change from the way the press celebrated the Curies when they won the Nobel Prize in 1903.

In December, Curie attended the Nobel Prize ceremony in Sweden. This was despite some people suggesting she shouldn't go because of the Langevin scandal. Back in France, the family stayed with friends to escape the journalists who were camped outside their house.

More health problems

Marie Curie was often away from home after winning her second Nobel Prize, looking for a health cure in the countryside. She had depression and kidney problems, and underwent a kidney operation in March 1912. Her children suffered as they were sent from one family member or governess to another. They hardly saw their mother for nearly a year.

Who's who

Hertha Ayrton
(1854–1923)

Hertha Ayrton was educated at home and was particularly good at maths. She is best known for her work investigating electric arcs and for the invention of the Ayrton Flapper Fan. The arc lamp was used in streetlights and many buildings, but the light often flickered and hissed. Ayrton's research suggested that if air was prevented from getting into the lamp, the problems would be solved. She became the first woman accepted into the Institution of Electrical Engineers, in 1899. The Ayrton Flapper Fan was used to clear trenches of poisonous gas during wartime.

Marie Curie was awarded an **honorary degree** at the University of Birmingham, England in September 1913. Sir Oliver Lodge, the head of the university, gave a speech at the presentation. He described Curie as "the greatest woman of science of all time".

In the summer of 1912, Curie was so ill she went to a **sanatorium** in the Savoie mountains, in the French Alps. When she felt better but not yet well enough to go home, she accepted an invitation to stay with her good friend Hertha Ayrton, a well-known British scientist who lived in Hampshire, England.

Irène and Ève joined their mother in September 1912. Ayrton tutored Irène and played piano with Ève. Ayrton inspired Irène on the subject of women's rights.

Return to normal life

Marie Curie finally returned to Paris in December and started making notes in her lab book for the first time in over a year. She also returned to her teaching job at the Sorbonne.

What did Marie Curie do during World War I?

The Radium Institute in Paris was finished in July 1914. It had been funded by the University of Paris and the Pasteur Foundation, mainly for Marie Curie's benefit. She ran the radioactivity laboratory there.

When the German army moved closer to Paris, Curie carried France's only supply of radium to Bordeaux, where the government had moved for the length of World War I (1914–1918). She had to take a 10-hour train journey but only stayed in Bordeaux one night before taking a military train back to Paris. Her team of researchers were fighting in the war, so work at the Institute was put on hold.

Mobile X-rays

In the meantime, Curie realized that X-rays could be extremely helpful to army doctors. The Red Cross made Curie head of its radiological service in 1914. During August and September, she set up places where X-rays could be used in the Paris area. These were run by volunteers who had been trained by Curie herself.

> "I soon found a field of activity [X-rays] which, once entered upon, absorbed the greatest part of my time and efforts until the end of the war, and even for some time thereafter..."
>
> Marie Curie

Curie then helped to develop and produce mobile radiography (X-ray) units to help doctors **diagnose** injuries at hospitals near the battlefront. She persuaded wealthy friends to give money and vehicles, and industries to hand over X-ray equipment. She then got car workshops to transform the vehicles into vans.

Marie Curie drove a petite Curie herself. They were used to provide X-ray equipment to hospitals around Paris.

Teaching herself

Curie had to learn to drive before she was able to operate the petite Curies. She also had to learn about anatomy (how the human body is made up) and how to use X-ray machines. Although she had taught students about X-rays, she had no experience of working with the machines herself.

PETITE CURIES

The mobile X-ray units were known as petite Curies – little Curies.

33

Irène and Marie Curie worked together at military hospitals to X-ray injured soldiers.

At the battlefront

In late October 1914, the first of 20 mobile X-ray units were sent to the battlefront. Curie travelled there with her daughter Irène (who was only 17) as her assistant. They worked together to X-ray injured soldiers, locating fractures, or cracks, in bones, as well as bullets.

Radon

In 1915, Curie brought back the radium from Bordeaux and used it to collect radon – a radioactive gas given out by radium. She had no protection from the radiation while doing this, and even carried the radium in her pockets, something we now know to be extremely dangerous. She used an electric pump to collect the gas in thin tubes about a centimetre long. Doctors then placed the tubes of radon in patients' bodies closest to where the radiation was needed to destroy tissue damaged by cancer.

Training

From 1916, Curie trained nurses and orderlies on how to use the X-ray machines. She set up courses at the Radium Institute and trained 150 women in X-ray technology.

"I am resolved to put all my strength at the service of my adopted country, since I cannot do anything for my unfortunate native country [Poland] just now..."

From a letter written by Marie to Paul Langevin, 1 January 1915

RADIOTHERAPY

Today, nearly half of all cancer sufferers have radiotherapy as part of their treatment to help cure their cancer. Doctors still use the same method used by doctors in Curie's day, which is known as internal radiotherapy. However, machines can now focus radiation beams onto the affected part of the body. This is called external radiotherapy. Both these methods try to shrink or destroy cancerous cells.

What did Marie Curie do after World War I?

Marie Curie's health was bad by this time. She had very poor eyesight, with double **cataracts** probably caused by radiation, and **anaemia** that left her feeling weak.

After the war, Curie continued to raise money for the Radium Institute, an activity she viewed as "wasted time" but one that was necessary for the Institute to continue running. The Curie Foundation – a centre for radiotherapy – was created in 1920 with money from the Lazard Brothers bank and French philanthropist Henri de Rothschild. Rothschild was fascinated by science and contributed money to many research projects. Curie continued to work in the lab, write scientific articles and organize the Institute.

Marie Curie was Director of Research at the Radium Institute in Paris.

Here is Marie Curie in her office at the Radium Institute.

Marie Curie and Missy

Many newspaper and magazine articles were written about Curie, including one in May 1920 that led to a Marie Curie Radium Campaign in the United States. The journalist was Marie Mattingly Maloney, known as Missy, editor of a US women's magazine. Curie complained to the journalist that US scientists had 50 grams (1.76 ounces) of radium for their research, but she had only slightly more than 1 gram (0.03 ounces). Missy vowed to raise money to buy more radium for Curie.

In her fundraising, Missy focused on radium as a cure for cancer in order to encourage people to give donations. It took just a year to raise enough money to buy a gram (0.03 ounces) of radium, which cost $100,000 (then equivalent to about £17,500). News of this campaign and that the US President would be handing over the radium changed how France saw Curie. She was back in the country's good books again.

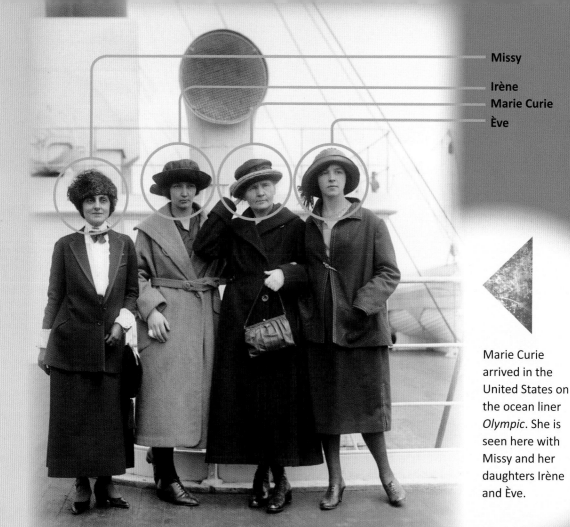

Missy
Irène
Marie Curie
Ève

Marie Curie arrived in the United States on the ocean liner *Olympic*. She is seen here with Missy and her daughters Irène and Ève.

The US tour

In 1921, along with her daughters, Curie travelled to the United States. They arrived in New York City on 11 May 1921. People had been waiting to see Curie for over five hours. A press conference took place before she even left the ship. It was all very different from France – in the United States, Curie was a celebrity.

The US visit included lectures, tours, dinners and a trip to the White House to meet Warren Harding, the US president. Harding handed over 1 gram (0.03 ounces) of radium to Curie. She was unable to take part in much of the rest of the tour because she was exhausted. She sent her daughters instead.

The trip was successful, not just because of the gift of radium. Curie was also given speaker's fees, equipment, other money raised by Missy and a deal to write a biography of Pierre Curie. Because of her work through the years, Curie had not spent a lot of time with her children, particularly Ève. The US trip, therefore, had another benefit – it allowed Curie's relationship with Ève to improve.

Marie Curie collected the radium from Warren Harding, the US president, on 20 May 1921.

Return to France

In February 1922, Curie became the first woman to be elected to the Academy of Medicine in France. It was a huge honour. On 26 December 1923, the 25th anniversary of the discovery of radium was celebrated at a party held at the Sorbonne. It was particularly special for Curie as her sisters and brother had travelled from Poland to be there.

What happened in the last years of Marie Curie's life?

In 1925, the first stone of the Radium Institute in Warsaw was laid by the Polish president. While Curie was thrilled that Poland finally had an Institute, she realized that there was not enough money to buy a constant supply of radium.

Both Curie and her sister Bronya had already used some of their savings to help pay for the Institute. So Curie went on another fundraising trip to the United States in October 1929. The price of radium had fallen by this time, so only $50,000 (then equivalent to about £8,000) was needed for 1 gram (0.03 ounces) of radium.

In 1929, on her second trip to the United States, Marie Curie travelled by train to Michigan.

By 1931, Marie's health was poor. However, she still attended scientific conferences that year.

Poor health

In the late 1920s, Curie's health deteriorated rapidly. She had to have four operations to fix the cataracts in her eyes. Sometimes she was so ill that she was unable to go to the lab. Instead, she worked at home, writing a book that was published after her death, called *Radioactivity*.

Marie Curie had a last holiday with her sister Bronya at Easter in 1934. In May, she went home from the lab feeling ill one day and never went back. The doctors couldn't work out what was wrong with her – some thought she had tuberculosis, the same disease her mother had died from. In fact, when Curie died on 4 July 1934, it was from a blood disorder called aplastic anaemia. It was a result of her working with radium over so many years. She was buried with Pierre Curie at Sceaux.

What was Marie Curie's legacy?

Marie Curie is known for her work on radioactivity, including her use of it as a way of discovering new elements. It was the basis of a new branch of science – atomic science, which focuses on atoms. Curie's discoveries also helped to change the way that serious diseases such as cancer are dealt with. Charities have been named after her, such as Marie Curie Cancer Care, which helps cancer sufferers to be cared for in their own homes. There are also many grants of money available in her name for scientific research projects.

An inspiring woman

Marie Curie is still the only woman to have won two Nobel Prizes. What's most amazing is that she achieved so much in the face of the world's negative views on women's abilities. Curie was not perfect, but she was extremely intelligent and hardworking. She had the strength of character to continue her work in the face of much criticism, some of which was aimed at her simply because she was a woman. She was determined to make a difference – and she did.

A new resting place

In April 1995, she was reburied – with Pierre Curie – at the Panthéon in Paris. The Panthéon is a place where the most famous heroes of France are buried. Above the entrance there is a sign saying, "For great men the grateful nation". She is the only woman to be buried there because of her life's work, not just because she was married to a well-known man. It shows just how important Marie Curie was to France and to the world.

Timeline

1867

Maria Sklodowska is born in Warsaw on 7 November

1883

Maria graduates top of her class from secondary school

1891

Maria begins studying at the Sorbonne in Paris, France, changing her name to Marie

1893

Marie gains her physics degree by graduating top of the class

1894

Marie gains her maths degree

1895

Marie marries Pierre Curie in July

1897

Marie Curie gives birth to her first daughter, Irène, in September

1898

The Curies publish the results of their research. They have discovered two new radioactive elements: polonium and radium.

1903

The Curies are joint winners with Henri Becquerel of the Nobel Prize in Physics

1904

Marie Curie gives birth to her second daughter, Ève, in December

1906

Pierre Curie dies in a road accident on 19 April

1911

Marie Curie wins the Nobel Prize in Chemistry

1914

In July, the Radium Institute opens in Paris, France

In October, Marie Curie provides X-ray machines, and training on how to use them, as her contribution to World War I

1921

Marie Curie and her daughters tour around the United States. Marie Curie is presented with 1 gram (0.03 ounces) of radium.

1929

Marie Curie travels to the United States again and returns with £8,000 ($50,000) to purchase 1 gram (0.03 ounces) of radium to give to the newly built Radium Institute in Warsaw, Poland

1934

Marie Curie dies of a blood disease on 4 July

Glossary

academy place of study

anaemia medical condition in which there are too few red cells in a person's blood. This means that the person is often pale and weak.

atom smallest part of an element that can exist on its own

cataracts medical condition in which the eyes become cloudy, resulting in poor or no eyesight

chemistry type of science that focuses on what things are made of and how substances react to each other

compound substance made of two or more separate elements

conference meeting of people interested in a particular subject; conferences are often held over a few days

current flow of electricity

degree course of study carried out at a university or other higher education institution

diagnose say what is wrong with a person's health

element substance that cannot be broken down into different substances by chemical means

governess in the past, a woman who taught children in their home

graduate to successfully finish a course of study, such as a degree at university

half-life time taken for the radioactivity of an element to fall to half its original value

honorary degree degree awarded to a person for his or her contribution to society, for example for scientific discovery

inspire create a positive feeling in someone, encouraging them to do something

isolate separate the pure form of something, for example separating an element from a compound

laboratory place where scientific experiments can be carried out

lecturer teacher at a college or university

mineral solid substance that is found in nature

nominate put forward a person's name for that person to win an award

philanthropist person who tries to help others, particularly by giving gifts of money

photographic plate sheet of metal or glass on which a photo can be developed

physics type of science that focuses on matter and energy, including heat, light, radiation, electricity, magnetism and atoms

professor highest rank of teacher in a university

radiation type of energy that moves from one place to another in the form of rays, waves or particles. Radiation can be used to treat some diseases, such as cancer.

radioactive giving out radiation

research investigate a subject in great detail, hoping to discover new information or ideas

sanatorium place where people suffering from long-term health problems go to rest and recover

tutor private teacher. A tutor usually goes to the pupil's home and teaches only one or a few children at a time.

X-ray high-energy wave that can pass through materials to show what is inside them. An X-ray of a body part shows the bones inside the body, which cannot normally be seen.

Find out more

Books

Marie Curie, Vicki Cobb (Dorling Kindersley, 2008)

Marie Curie, Philip Steele (QED, 2014)

Marie Curie (Scientists Who Made History), Liz Gogerly (Wayland, 2014)

Websites

www.bbc.co.uk/history/historic_figures/curie_marie.shtml
This BBC web page has basic information about Marie Curie's life.

**www.sciencemuseum.org.uk/onlinestuff/stories/marie_curie_and_the_
history_of_radioactivity.aspx**
Learn more about Marie Curie and radioactivity on the Science Museum's
website. You could also visit the museum to see some of the objects that she
used in her experiments.

Further research

- See if you can find out more about the scientists who attended the Solvay
  Conference in 1911.

- What did Ève Curie do for a living?

- Try to find out about the history of Poland, particularly around the time of
  Marie Curie's birth.

- Investigate the many products made from radium before scientists realized
  how dangerous it was to people's health.

Index

atomic science 42
atoms 13
Ayrton, Hertha 30, 31
Ayrton Flapper Fan 30

Becquerel, Henri 12, 13, 18, 19
Bouchard, Charles 18
Branly, Édouard 26, 27

cancer treatment 4, 35, 37, 42
Carnegie, Andrew 25
chalcolite 15
compounds 13, 14, 25
Curie, Ève 21, 23, 31, 38, 39
Curie, Jacques 13, 22
Curie, Marie
  children 11, 21, 23, 25, 30, 38, 39
  death of 41
  diary 22, 25
  Director of Research at the Radium Institute 32, 36, 37
  doctorate 12, 21
  early life 6–7
  education 6, 7–9
  elected to French Academy of Medicine 39
  English honorary degree 31
  family background 6, 7
  health problems 17, 28, 30–31, 36, 41
  marries Pierre Curie 11
  Nobel Prizes 4, 18, 29, 42
  Sorbonne professor 22, 24, 31
  US tours 38–39, 40
  war work 32–35
  widow 22

Curie, Pierre 10–11, 13, 14, 17, 18, 19, 21, 22, 24, 39, 41, 42
Curie Foundation 36
Curie measurement for radium 28
Curie Scholarships 25

Einstein, Albert 28, 29
electric arcs 30
elements 13, 14, 15, 17, 25

First World War 32–35
French Academy of Medicine 39
French Academy of Sciences 26–27

girls' education 4, 6, 8

half-life 17
Harding, Warren 38, 39

isolation of elements 15, 17

Joliot-Curie, Irène 4, 11, 23, 31, 34, 35, 38

Kelvin, Lord 25

Langevin, Paul 28, 29
Lodge, Sir Oliver 31

Maeterlinck, Maurice 29
Maloney, Marie Mattingly (Missy) 37, 38, 39
Marconi, Guglielmo 26
Marie Curie Cancer Care 42
Marie Curie Radium Campaign 37
Mittag-Leffler, Magnus Goesta 19

mobile radiography units 33, 35
Nobel, Alfred 18
Nobel Prizes 4, 18, 29, 42

Panthéon 4, 42
Pasteur Foundation 32
patents 20
petite Curies 33
pitchblende 15
Planck, Max 29
Poincaré, Henri 17, 28
polonium 4, 14, 15, 17, 18

radioactivity 4, 13, 14, 17, 19, 25, 29, 32, 42
radiotherapy 35, 36
radium 4, 14, 15, 17, 18, 20, 25, 28, 32, 35, 37, 38, 39, 40, 41
Radium Institute, Paris 32, 35, 36, 37
Radium Institute, Warsaw 40
radon 35
Red Cross 32
Roentgen, Wilhelm 12
Rothschild, Henri de 36
Rutherford, Ernest 29

Solvay Conference 28–29
Sorbonne 4, 9, 17, 22, 24, 31, 39

thorium 14

United States 37–39, 40
uranium 12, 13, 14, 19

wireless telegraphy 26
women's rights 31

X-rays 12, 19, 32, 33, 34, 35